Purple Orchids

Purple Orchids
by Ashish
Paperback Edition

First Published in 2023 by

Inkfeathers Publishing
Vivek Vihar, New Delhi 110095
www.inkfeathers.com

ISBN 978-81-19483-04-4

Purple Orchids

Ashish

Inkfeathers Publishing
www.inkfeathers.com

Preface

In the realm of youth, relationships often flicker like candle flames, casting a transient glow before extinguishing in the winds of change. As teenagers, we tend to approach relationships with a sense of lightness, believing that if one doesn't work out, we can easily move on to another. We embark on a journey of exploration, anticipating that love and connection will simply fall into place. Little do we realise that this journey is fraught with complexities and consequences.

But then, amidst the ebb and flow of life's uncertainties, there comes a pivotal moment—one fine day when everything changes. It is on this fateful day that we meet someone who captivates our hearts, someone who resonates with us in ways we never thought possible. We feel an inexplicable connection, a warmth that envelops us, and a profound sense of well-being that permeates our souls. We get closer, and the phases of a relationship unfold before us.

This book, "Purple Orchids," is an earnest expression of a realisation that was bestowed upon me by someone special. As a young man, I confess to having made countless mistakes, seldom pondering their impact. However, this book is not a lamentation of regrets but rather an ode to the happy regrets—the regrets that fostered profound realisations and fuelled personal growth. It is a heartfelt acknowledgment, a thank-you letter to that one person who opened my eyes and made me see.

For me, the path to understanding was not an easy one. I eventually grasped the importance of cherishing love, but not without a cost that forever remains etched in my heart. This book encapsulates the weight of that cost—the poignant reminder of the sacrifices made, and the lessons learned. It is a testament to the profound impact that a single individual can have on our lives, altering our perceptions and guiding us towards self-discovery.

While I have previously penned stories for films, writing a book, let alone sharing my innermost thoughts and vulnerabilities, is a new endeavour for me. I embark upon this literary journey with trepidation and hope, weaving words that bear the weight of my experiences and emotions. It is my sincerest desire that you, the reader, will find solace, inspiration, and perhaps even a glimpse of your own journey within these pages.

So, with an open heart and a sincere intention, I invite you to join me on this poignant expedition through the maze of youthful relationships. May this book serve as a reminder to cherish the connections we forge, to embrace the growth that accompanies our mistakes, and to appreciate the individuals who leave an indelible mark upon our hearts.

With gratitude and anticipation.

1.0

YEARNING EYES

In the last year of college, my eyes sought you,
Mornings brimmed with motivation anew.
In the cafeteria, we talked, two worlds apart,
Yet our gazes met, connecting heart to heart.
Those sharp eyes pierced my soul, oh so deep,
I knew I wanted by them each morning to sleep.
Falling in love, a silent dance we shared,
Dreaming of waking up, in your eyes ensnared.

2.0

SILENT DIALOUGES

We rarely spoke, yet our hearts conversed,
Silent dialogue, love's language immersed.
Our eyes engaged in heartfelt exchange,
As love flowed freely, emotions rearranged.
Amidst friends, eating pizza at Andaz Delhi,
Our eyes wove a tale, words unspoken, set free.
That conversation through our eyes remains,
A cherished memory, where love forever reigns.

3.0

SPIRITUALITY IN A SHADY HOTEL

In souls' embrace, trust gently grew,
A spiritual connection, both felt true.
In a shady hotel, college bunked away,
Love's realm engulfed; in passion we sway.
Tears flowed, a shared moment divine,
Lost pigeons found; past lives align.

4.0

AN ANGEL

Scared and short on funds, I took a leap,
Arranging finances, sigh of relief I keep.
Knowing your love for pets, I took a chance,
Bringing home Dooby, a brown beagle's dance.
With shining eyes, he made us feel whole,
Love's trinity formed, in our hearts' console.

5.0

LONG AWAITED HUG

In knowing you, the child within came alive,
In the right mindset, I sought you, strive by strive.
Amidst lockdown's grasp, rules I dared to break,
For your eyes and touch, risks I chose to take.
Long had it been since our souls embraced,
That hug etched in memory; love's warmth traced.

6.0

THE WRONG GUIDANCE

In the wrong guidance, love's pillars shook,
Fooled and misled, my judgment mistook.
Though I loved you, doubts crept within,
Temptations whispered, desires to spin.
I apologise for being a fool,
Not heeding my heart, straying from love's rule.
Lessons learned, I see the truth at last,
Regretting the past, a chance to rebuild, steadfast.

7.0

SORRY PT 1

Unaware and misguided, my brain's sway,
Temptations lured, led astray each day.
Yet you stood by me, unwavering and strong,
Unhealed from the past, I caused you wrong.
I now see the pain I made you endure,
Apologies pour forth, sincere and pure.
In the HOLY name, forgive me, my dear,
Yearning to stop time, mend what's held dear.

8.0

LOVER'S MELODY

In dreams, I close my eyes and see you,
Puffy cheeks, soft lips, eyes shining true,
Retina's sparkle, brows that frame your face,
Thick black hair, a beauty I can't erase.
With earphones on, I long for your voice,
Melodies of love, my heart's rejoice.
Through battles fought and cuddles sought,
In your embrace, love's warmth is taught.

9.0

SWEET DESIRES IN HEAVEN

Oh, V! your hands weave magic. It's true,
Your vanilla buttercream cake, a dream come true.
As my wife, I long to call you one day,
To kiss your tired hands on a rainy day.
Endless love, I promise when you're in need,
Though I lost you in this life, paradise we'll succeed.

10.0

RELEASE FOR HAPPINESS

In love's embrace, I set you free,
For your happiness, my heart agrees.
I'll gladly watch you with someone new,
As long as he sees the real you.
Though your heart wanders far and wide,
I know our love has softly sighed.
But fear not, I'll still be near,
A call away when you need me, my dear.

11.0

FLY HIGH

In realms above, where whiteness gleams,
You and I shall meet, beyond earthly schemes,
No boundaries bind, nor past's weight to bear,
Just pure freedom, suspended in air.
Together we'll soar, our spirits set free,
Dreaming of a day when we'll fly as three.

12.0

SORRY 2.0

In scars of a lifetime, my deeds reside,
Five years of yearning, I now confide,
I failed to hear, your voice so true,
Motherly embrace, you always knew.
Hurt I inflicted, beyond measure and depth,
Love overflowing, your heart never left,
You crossed limits, protecting our bond,
Forgive my blindness, I now respond.
Each second of hurt, I deeply regret,
Taking you for granted, my greatest debt,
With humble plea, forgiveness I implore,
For love so profound, forevermore.

13.0

AURA

In your presence, a sight so endearing,
A birthmark on your nostril appearing,
Uncommon yet charming, a mark so unique,
When you wear a bindi, your beauty reaches its peak,
And those thin earrings, they capture my view,
My lips resist temptation, admiring you.

14.0

RAIN AND YOU

You and rain, forever intertwined,
In my heart, a place uniquely defined.
Underneath its tears, our memories bloom,
In a hidden spot, where love found its room.
As the drops fell, we shared a sweet kiss,
That feeling, etched in my soul's abyss.
Now you're gone, and sorrow fills the air,
Does the rain weep for what's no longer there?
Is it you, my love, returning in disguise,
Or the almighty shedding tears from the skies?
Lost in longing, I seek solace in the rain,

Hoping it washes away this heartache and pain.
But deep within, I know it's just a dream,
Raindrops can't bring back what once did gleam.
Yet, in this downpour, I'll find strength to cope,
For within its rhythm, I'll heal and find hope.

15.0

ONE LAST TIME

What we had was precious and true,
A transformation from boy to man, thanks to you.
Oh darling, you made me believe in love,
And now, I long for you, my turtledove.
Forgive me, darling, for my past mistakes,
Just give me your hand, for old times' sake.
Let me embrace you for one last time,
And feel your lips against mine, sublime.

16.0

DON'T LET IT FADE

I messed it up, I know, my dear,
Your longing for a love sincere.
You say it wasn't your right place,
Yet years we spent, face to face.
Your love for me still shines so bright,
But now you're leaving, taking flight.
Can't we mend what's been torn apart?
I've seen my flaws, felt my guilt-ridden heart.
I recognise the pain I caused,
Ghosted you, left you feeling lost.
My apologies, mere words they may be,
But for once, let me keep you safe; you'll see.

In my arms, let love's warmth embrace,
Just once, let me cherish your grace.
For I've come to know the mistakes I've made,
And I'm begging for a chance, don't let it fade.
Together we've shared so much it's true,
Please give me one more chance with you.
I'll make it right, I swear, my dove,
For once, let me show you the depths of my love.

17.0

TRICKED

In the realm of misunderstanding, my dear,
I never wished your friendships to disappear.
Nor did I request your social ties to sever,
Yet blame finds its way, like a persistent endeavor.
Perhaps deceived by whispers, you now sway,
But now, my sweet, I never led you astray.

18.0

THE MASK

On every special occasion, I stood by your side,
Meeting those dear to you, with social awkwardness, I tried.
I know how to act, I wear a mask so well,
Yet you worry about future events, where I'll dwell.
But honey, your point is baseless, I've proven my care,
In every moment with you, I've always been there.

19.0

SORRY 3.0

In this relationship, I confess my flaw,
A kid at heart, my immaturity did gnaw.
My foolish decisions caused you much pain,
Disrespecting you, my actions were in vain.
Words uttered in anger hold no true weight,
I see now, it was wrong, a bitter debate.
The guy you met, calm and peaceful inside,
You relished in fights, so I tried to abide.
I apologise for crossing boundaries and more,
As a boyfriend, I faltered, left you sore.

But trust these realisations, genuine and sincere,
Let me offer you love, let me wipe away each tear.
I long to be better, to show you my growth,
To cherish your heart and make amends, both.
With newfound maturity, I'll strive to be kind,
Let me offer you love and bring back the smile you find.

20.0

FAMILY TIES

In family's embrace, your name did reside,
I dreamed of marrying you, side by side,
I raised you up, like my dear mother true,
Yet, sorrow struck, as hearts were torn in two.
My mother's love for you, it knows no end,
She longs for you, as a lost daughter, friend,
The family saw in you a gem so rare,
Oh, how I mourn the loss, burden hard to bear?
You, the sole girl who entered my abode,
Never before had friends met my own fold,
Regret consumes me, forgiveness I seek,
For losing you, my heart feels truly weak.

21.0

COME BACK HOME

In your absence, I long for your touch,
Your voice, your eyes—I miss them so much.
Yearning to hear you call my name,
Grant me one chance, love, to reclaim,
I'll shatter barriers, keep you close and warm,
No demands, just be here let me transform.
Trust me, my love, in this plea, I confide,
For together, let's mend what's been untied.

22.0

BLAME ME

In silence, my mind rests, but my heart aches,
Years slipping away, don't let them forsake.
I'm sorry, misunderstood, the blame misplaced,
Society's judgment, a girl's dreams erased.
Yearning for fruitfulness, she longs to create,
Yet the boy they raised; society fears to berate.

23.0

WHAT AN ACTOR

In the realm of love, a tangled plight I find,
How can I seek another with you in my mind?
Your thoughts embrace me as I slumber deep,
And greet me upon the morn, when waking from sleep.
I yearn to distance, to break this binding chain,
Yet your presence persists, causing sweetest pain.
My heart may weep in solitary hours alone,
Yet my eyes, in joy, a different tale has shown.
An actor of emotions, on life's grand stage,
I perform with artistry, concealing love's wage.
For in my mind and heart, you firmly reside,
A haunting presence I can't escape, nor hide.

24.0

SILENT DESIRE'S

I wanna kiss you, make you feel alright,
In your battles, I'll stand up and fight.
Weary eyes, tired of endless cries,
I crave your presence, in my arms, my prize.
Alone, I wander, weakened by your absence,
As if my soul has left, in silence's essence.
But with you near, I find solace anew,
Together we conquer our love ever true.

25.0

CALMNESS AROUND YOU

Just for once, see through my eyes,
Where the moon bears scars but you've none, oh love,
Forgive me for gazing at you,
Your words bring serenity, a tranquil balm,
In your presence, I find solace profound,
With you around, my restless heart is bound.

26.0

YOU WERE SPECIAL

On 25th August, a memory unfolds,
You made it special, or so it goes,
Your presence, a light that filled my day,
Turning a boy's whims into a man's display.
Now I stand here, knowing I'll miss you,
In life's precious moments, old and new,
Though I blamed you once for joy's decay,
In hindsight, fault rests on my own dismay.
I made you stand in shadows of despair,
While you sought brightness, I wasn't aware,
Regret fills my heart, a somber tune,

For I should have embraced you under the moon.
But now, dear one, the time has passed,
I hope you find happiness, forever to last,
In memories we shared, bittersweet and true,
I bid farewell, knowing I'll miss you.

27.0

GOD'S PRESENT

Since childhood, I longed for true love's embrace,
yearning for a hand to hold at day's end.
Finally, I discovered my love language—a tight hug
and a gentle grasp. Thankfully, God blessed me,
and there you were, a precious gift. I, the fool,
failed to realise that the priceless treasure was mine
all along.

28.0

MOOD SWINGS

In words unspoken, emotions swirl and sway,
Lost between sorrow and joy's gentle play.
Silent echoes linger, I search for a way,
To bridge the divide, our paths in disarray.
Will fate reunite us, in destiny's design?
Or shall we drift apart, like stars in decline?
Questions unanswered, yet hope intertwines,
Whispering softly, our futures may align.
I yearn to know, if time will allow,
Another encounter, a shared moment's vow.
But for now, I'll hold this yearning at bay,
In the realm of uncertainty, I'll learn to stay.

29.0

THE SACRIFICES YOU MADE

In days of old, I recall a sight so dear,
How you concealed tears, away from my view,
Outside the window, masking pain, my dear,
So, I wouldn't witness your anguish, true.
Through my troubled times, you thought of me,
Withholding your worries, for my relief,
Oh, love, your sacrifices, abundantly,
I'm sorry, as a lover, I've been a thief.
A wretched soul, I turned, inhumanly,
Unaware of the gem that dwelled besides,
But when you departed, I truly could see,
The worth of your presence once denied.
Regret now fills my heart, heavy and deep,
For losing your love, the loss I now weep.

30.0

I STOLE

Hey, do you remember when I came to see you?
And Dooby, the way he ate the watermelon, too.
At that moment, I glimpsed something true,
A special sparkle within your eyes, warmth grew.
You were complete, radiant and so glad,
I witnessed your joy; it made my heart glad.
How do I forgive myself for stealing away
That sense of completeness, for causing dismay?
How do I forgive for not seeing you,
For keeping you in the shadows, it's true.
Now, I surrender my heart to the Almighty's might,
Hoping forgiveness will come, bringing back the light.

31.0

BROKEN TRUST

One night I sat, pondering in despair,
Knowing God's punishment soon would be there,
Deep in my heart, the guilt firmly resided,
For introducing the third one, love divided.
I distanced from you, drawn close to another,
Leaving you unseen, waiting for the other,
Truth revealed, our world shattered, aghast,
Begging forgiveness, received after a week's vast.
Yet the void within you, still stood tall,
I vowed no more glimpses of your past's call,
But a fool, I repeated the mistake anew,
Different faces, same error, tears ensued.

Questions arise, am I a girl gone astray?
Or simply not interesting, a thought's disarray?
I apologise, my love, for my self-absorbed art,
Toxicity consumed, the third shattered our heart.
Cheating, trust-breaking, a vile deed I've done,
Surely God's wrath, my punishment begun,
Nightly tears flow, for you're no longer near,
Remorse-filled, I weep, my soul drenched in fear.

32.0

SORRY 4.0

Don't go right now, stay here one last time,
Let's fall in love, one more time, sublime.
I need you by my side, please don't depart,
Begging you, pleading, let love restart.
I'm a new man now, changed and grown,
No longer a boy, as you've always known.
I'm sorry, so sorry, don't leave me alone,
Without you, I can't breathe, my heart's overthrown.
How could I be so foolish, I've lost you somehow,
In disbelief, I wonder, "How? Oh, how?"
Just grant me one wish, don't say love is gone,
For without your love, my world is withdrawn.

33.0

WE DEM BOYS

Oh, my champ, oh my boy,
Boys are the best, boys are cool, boys are perfect.
But wait, boys can be such dumbfucks,
Foolish and blind, thinking so highly of themselves.
They realize the worth and pain,
Only when it's gone, when it's lost.
Oh, boys, learn to appreciate,
Before it's too late, at any cost.

34.0

SWEET DREAMS

In absence, my love, you may not be near,
Yet let my affection span beyond time's sphere.
Within my dreams, I'll hold you close, my dear,
Guarding your heart from this world's fears severe.
Allow my love to endure, unwavering and true,
Forever, in my dreams, I'll be with you.

35.0

SUNSIGN

In stars we sought our fates, just for fun,
Capricorn and Virgo, two as one.
Ninety-three percent, our compatibility score,
Now I see, it's not what it was before.
Foolishly I believed, part of the lucky few,
But alas, I'm in the 7%, and I rue.

36.0

PAPA JI

In your father's presence, they all grew quiet,
But as an actor, I dared to ignite.
With courage in my heart, I freely stood,
Tricking him with a smile, as he misunderstood.
That look on his face, a moment of surprise,
A funny memory cherished, where laughter lies.

37.0

PERSONALITY CHANGE

In shadows of truth, I struggle to believe,
Those words you uttered, a bitter reprieve,
A relationship untangled, slipping away,
Yet I can't deny, no one deserves this dismay.
For the way I treated you, a grievous sin,
Regret now consumes, as I yearn to begin,
Trust me, dear heart, the old self is no more,
Each day, I evolve, a calmness I restore.
Like a child rediscovered, love I embrace,
Growing, transforming, with gentle grace,
No longer the one who caused you to weep,
I'm changing, evolving, in promises I'll keep.

38.0

DARKNESS

Amidst my flaws, mistakes were made,
Your shattered heart, my debts unpaid.
I failed to see the love you deserved,
But in my darkness, I was observed.
Though you're gone, I'll pray each day,
For the chance to mend and find our way.

39.0

I KNOW I FUCKED UP

Hey, I know I fucked up, I could've been better,
Missing you now, my heart feels so much lighter.
It's strange how love keeps us consumed all day,
But when you're gone, I ponder my role and ways.
Thoughts echo regrets, how I could've been more,
As a partner, a lover, my soul deeply sore.
But in the silence, I learn from my mistake,
Growing stronger, wiser, for the love's sake.
Though you're not here, I carry the weight,
Reflecting on past, seeking a better fate.
I miss you dearly, yet I'll strive to improve,
For love's lessons teach us how to truly groove.

40.0

BAD DAYS MAKES ME MISS YOU MORE

In moments of darkness, I yearn to connect,
To hold you close, your presence to protect.
Through these tough times, memories ensue,
Your touch, your warmth, a love that's true.
A taste of your cake, a sweet embrace,
Longing for you, in this lonely space.

41.0

LAST HUG

In echoes of our past, I find regret's touch,
If realisations bloomed a little sooner, as such,
We'd laugh at the irony, with hearts set free,
Oh, how I yearn for the days when you were mine, V.
A purple orchid's sight stirs a longing inside,
I wish you were here, walking by my side,
To gift you those petals, a daily display,
But distance and time have taken you away.

I yearn to embrace you, in love's sweet embrace,
Just like that last time, when we faced our fate,
Knowing our paths would diverge, we'd journey alone,
The road from the mall, etched with emotions unknown.
V, oh V, how I miss you, my dear,
The ache in my heart whispers crystal clear,
Memories of us linger, too painful to bear,
I long for your presence, I miss you way too much.

42.0

LET'S RISE FROM GTHE ASHES

You saw the worst phase of me, unsettled and lost,
Dreams filled my brain; reality was the cost.
Yearning to earn, to provide for our kin,
I sought success, let curiosity win.
With all I had, I tried to invest,
Hoping for fortunes, putting it to the test.
But heartbreak ensued, as I earned a mere sum,
Eight hundred bucks, a bitter outcome.
You witnessed my anguish, judged me astray,
But now I'm settled, I see my mistakes in full display.
I apologise sincerely, without a pause or delay,

Knowing I hurt you, I've learned a better way.
Once past that phase, no repeat of that strife,
I admit my fault, ready to pay with my life.
Punish, scold, even slap, if it eases your pain,
But stay by my side, through this rough terrain.
For I believe in us, our love's enduring grace,
If we conquer this hurdle, we'll find an embrace.
I promise you, together we'll become the best,
Rising from the ashes, surpassing any test.

43.0

LOST LOVE

You blame me for the loss of those you held dear,
Yet I never asked you to shun friends, I fear.
I planned a grand surprise on your special day,
But your pals craved beer, so the plan did sway.
Though I felt remorse, I concealed my dismay,
For your joy mattered most, so I let it sway.
In silence, I endured the ache that I felt,
Holding back my desire to bid you farewell.
Yes, I once fell out of love's tender embrace,
But with patience and effort, love I did trace.
I'll keep on falling, surrendering my heart,
For the feeling of love with you, I'll never part.
So, know, my dear, I'll forever hold it true,
The yearning for love, twice, I'll always miss you.

44.0

THE WRONG GUY

In maturity's embrace, your heart resides,
Kindness flows through you, like gentle tides.
With intellect's fire, your mind soars high,
Yet in love's labyrinth, you chose to try.
A life endured with struggles, battles fought,
But in the wrong guy's arms, your heart was caught.

45.0

COME BACK HOME

You say you love me, but trust's undone,
Fair enough, doubts cast their shadow, run,
Yet pause, consider my journey's toil,
0.5 percent, a slice of love's soil.
Think of the man, working on himself,
Confident strides, his heart on the shelf,
I know emotions sway, stray from our dream,
But ponder the one who fell twice, it seems.

46.0

SWITCHED OUR ROLES

I remember when you craved pizza's zest,
While I devoured burgers with a zest.
But now I see you've switched your role,
Embracing burgers with a hearty soul.
Oh, how time flies, memories so sweet,
Our roles reversed, a change complete.

47.0

YOU DESERVED BETTER

In years entwined, we sought to bridge the divide,
You, tireless, tore down walls, side by side.
Through good and bad, when skies were grey,
You stayed, unfaltering, every step of the way.
In moments low, when shadows cast their spell,
You held on, hoping my heart would mend and swell.
Yet I, in my folly, added bricks with naught but shame,
Disregarding your soul, tarnishing our flame.
Oh, my love, you merit a nobler soul than mine,
A partner who cherishes, a love that will shine.
I admit my immaturity, my flaws, my plea,
You deserve better, my darling, can't you see?

48.0

ONE LAST CHANCE MAYBE?

You deserve better, more than I've been,
Give me another chance; let redemption begin.
This one last plea, I promise no regret,
A different person, I've changed, don't forget.
I understand your doubts, your lack of belief,
But trust in this divine force, it's beyond my grief.
We both seek to move forward, to embrace the new,
But baby, grant me this last chance, I'll forever stay true.
I won't let go, I'll never leave your side,
Together we'll conquer, our love will abide.
One final time, let's make our hearts mend,
And in this journey, our souls forever blend.

49.0

YOU

I just can't stop thinking about you,
In my dreams, you visit, so true.
Your voice echoes in my mind,
Waking up, I hope to find,
Your presence near, my heart yearns.
Longing to embrace, my soul burns.
But how can I find peace of mind,
When guilt consumes, so unkind?
I shattered you, a painful deed,
Leaving my heart in dire need.

Forgive me, for I am sorry,
My love for you remains unwary.
In every minute, thoughts run deep,
Aching body, no solace to keep.
Laughter escapes, burdened by pain,
Lost you, my love, it's hard to explain.
How will my heart ever mend?
When you're so far, my dearest friend.
I just can't stop thinking about you,
Forever sorry, my love is true.

50.0

GOODBYE V

My heart aches while I write this last poem,
So much to say, yet I've said enough, I know.
But remember, I'll be waiting for you,
On that blessed day, when our love will shine through.
Ring the bell of my house on Sunday morn,
My mother awaits you, downstairs, all adorned.
In my dreams, I weep as you grace the scene,
In a white saree, our union, a love so serene.
I promised a closure, with confidence anew,
But now I see, I don't need it, it's true.
I'll cherish these memories, live with thoughts so dear,
A part of me forever loves you, my dear.

I'll miss you deeply, that much is clear,
Time may pass, but my love won't disappear.
Don't hold back return when you're ready,
Know that I'll be waiting, my love steady.
May you find the best in life's every test,
Become a baker, the finest and the blessed.
Tears stream down as I bid you farewell,
We can mend it, though the journey is hard to tell.
Goodbye, my love, I'll miss you, it's true,
But I must walk this path, painful but new.
Remember, my heart holds a space just for you,
Take your time, come back, our love will renew.

www.ingramcontent.com/pod-product-compliance
Lightning Source LLC
LaVergne TN
LVHW052056160826
845678LV00015B/3260

* 9 7 8 8 1 1 9 4 8 3 0 4 4 *